KIDS' PROJECTS
FOR
RAINY DAYS

TORMONT

Acknowledgements
The publisher would like to thank the following contributors
for their help in the production of this book: Clare Beaton,
Cheryl Brown, Joan Jones and Anita Ruddell; and also the staff
and children of Riversdale Primary School.

This edition published in 1998 by
Tormont Publications Inc.
338 Saint Antoine St. East
Montreal, Canada H2Y 1A3
Tel. (514) 954-1441
Fax (514) 954-5086

Project editor: Cheryl Brown
Book design: Anita Ruddell
Cover design: Zapp
Photography: Jon Bouchier

Printed in China

Contents

Remember

- Wear an apron and cover the work area.
- Collect together the items in the "Materials" box at the beginning of each project.
- Always ask an adult for help when you see this sign ⚠
- Clean up after yourself.

Play Dough Fun

Play dough is quick and easy to make, but as it involves cooking you will need to ask a grown-up to help you.

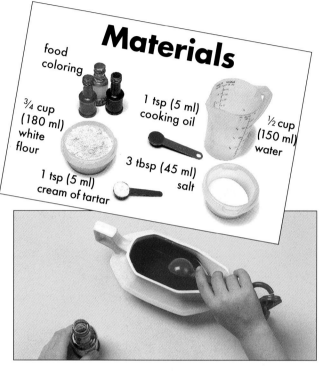

Materials

food coloring

¾ cup (180 ml) white flour

1 tsp (5 ml) cooking oil

½ cup (150 ml) water

3 tbsp (45 ml) salt

1 tsp (5 ml) cream of tartar

1 Put the flour, salt, cream of tartar and cooking oil into a saucepan and stir together.

2 Add 1-2 teaspoonfuls (5-10 ml) of red food coloring to the water and stir well. The more you add the deeper the color will be.

3 Gradually add the water to the other ingredients, mixing thoroughly to remove any lumps.

⚠ **4** Cook over a low to medium heat. Stir continuously until the dough becomes thick and leaves the sides of the pan almost clean.

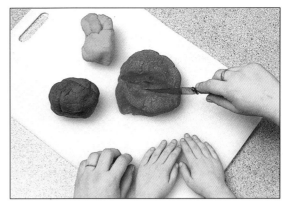

! **5** Scrape the mixture from the saucepan onto a smooth flat surface. Put the saucepan in to soak immediately. Make up two more batches of blue and yellow play dough.

! **6** Leave the play dough to cool for at least ten minutes. Before using the dough, ask an adult to cut through it with a knife to test that the inside has cooled too.

7 Knead the cooled play dough until it becomes smooth and pliable. You can mix the three colors to get a marbled effect.

8 You can make up a variety of colors by mixing together red, yellow and blue.
Red and yellow makes orange.
Blue and yellow makes green.
Red and blue makes purple.

STORAGE TIP
Roll the play dough up into balls of the same color. Wrap each in plastic and keep in an air-tight container in the refrigerator.

Salt Dough Medallions

Salt dough can be baked hard, painted and varnished so that you can keep the things you make forever.

Materials

ribbon

gold paper

1 tsp (5 ml) cooking oil

¾ cup (180 ml) white flour

⅓ cup (80 ml) water

3 tbsp (45 ml) salt

1 Mix together the salt, flour and cooking oil in a bowl. Add the water a little at a time and mix to a smooth paste that leaves the sides of the bowl clean.

2 Place the dough onto a lightly-floured board. Use a lightly-floured rolling pin to roll out the dough to about ¼ inch (½ cm) thick.

3 Use cookie cutters to cut out several shapes from the salt dough.

4 Use a paper clip to print a pattern on the medallions.

! **5** Open out the paper clip and prick out a circular pattern on the medallions. Place them onto a greased baking tray and bake in a preheated oven at 250°F (120°C) until they are firm (about 2 hours).

! **6** Remove the medallions from the oven and leave to cool. Paint and lightly varnish. Decorate the medallions. To make a winner's medal, cut a star from gold paper and glue onto the center of one of the medallions.

7 Overlap the ends of the ribbon and glue together. Glue the medallion firmly to the overlapped ends of the ribbon.

The medallions can easily be changed into badges by simply taping a safety pin to the back of the decorated shapes.

Materials

ribbon

salt dough

felt

material

2 pieces of pipe cleaner

Faces on the Door

Follow the instructions for making salt dough on page 6, then use it to model these funny faces to hang over your bedroom door.

1 Lightly flour your hands and a board. Knead the dough on the board until it is smooth. Break off a small piece and put to one side.

2 Press the larger ball of dough into a face shape about ½ inch (1 cm) thick. To make the eyes and mouth, press a pencil into the face.

3 Break the remaining dough into two and shape a nose and a mustache. Use a little water to lightly wet the back of each piece and position onto the face.

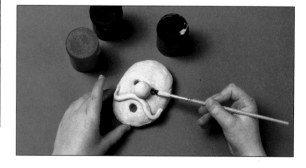

! **4** Bake in a preheated oven on a greased baking tray at 250°F (120°C) for 3-4 hours until firm. When cool, paint and varnish.

5 Cut an eye patch and band from the felt. Position on the face and secure with glue at the back of the head.

6 Make an earring by twisting a pipe cleaner into a circle. Glue to the side of the pirate's head.

7 Wrap the material around the pirate's head and secure on one side with the other pipe cleaner. Glue the finished head onto a long piece of ribbon.

Hang the completed faces on your closet or bedroom doors. You could model smaller faces and hang these from drawers.

Teddy Bear Pencil Holder

This cute bear can be hung up on the wall or pinned onto a notice board.

Materials

material

construction paper

ribbon

1 Trace the teddy bear patterns on pages 43-44 onto a piece of construction paper and cut out.

2 Use felt-tip pens to color in the bear's eyes, nose and mouth. Staple the head to the body.

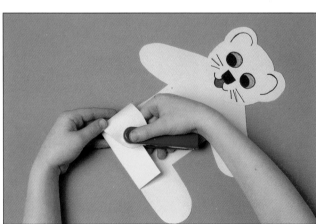

3 Fold up the flap at the bottom of the body. Fold the legs inwards over the flap. Staple each leg to the flap to make a pocket.

4 Fold the bear's arms inwards and staple together.

5 Cut 2 bows from the material and glue over the staples.

6 Cut a piece of construction paper 5 by 6½ inches (12 cm x 16 cm), roll up into a tube and staple in place.

7 Tape a ribbon loop to the back of the bear's head to hang it up with. Push the tube down between the paws.

Now slip some colored pencils or felt-tip pens into the tube. For Halloween make a black cat holder. For Easter make a rabbit holder and fill it with chocolate eggs.

Materials

wrapping paper

round plastic bottle

strips of crêpe paper

box

6 garden sticks

colored paper

Ringo

Make this game for a brother or sister, then play it together to see who can get the best score.

1 Choose a wrapping paper with a repeat pattern and cut out 6 figures from it. Glue these onto colored paper and cut around the outline.

2 Tape each figure to the top of a garden stick.

3 Cover the box with wrapping paper.

! 4 Poke 6 holes through the top of the box, spacing them out evenly.

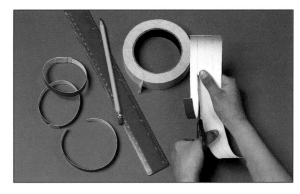

5 Use a coin or small bottle lid to trace 6 circles from the colored paper. Cut out and number them 1 to 6. Glue a number next to each hole.

6 Cut open a round plastic bottle. Cut 6 ½-inch (1-cm) strips from the plastic. Tape the strips into rings.

7 Wind the strips of crêpe paper around the rings until the plastic is completely covered. Secure the ends of the paper with tape.

Push the sticks into the holes. Take turns to see how many figures you can score. The first one to reach 50 is the winner.

Butterfly Card

An unusual card that is a present too.

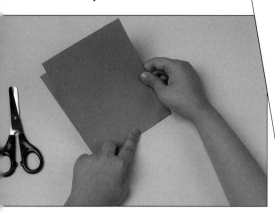

Materials

ribbon

safety pin

sticky pad

colored paper

wrapping paper

foil tape

sequins

glitter

1 Cut a piece of paper 12 by 5 inches (30 cm x 12 cm). Fold in half.

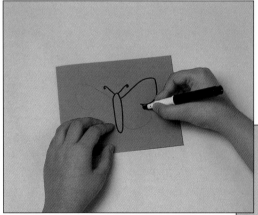

2 Trace the butterfly pattern (page 43) onto the front of the card.

3 Draw around the outline of the butterfly with a black felt-tip pen. Decorate the body.

!4 Cut around the outside of the butterfly wings and lift up.

5 Cut a piece of colored paper 5½ by 4 inches (13 cm x 10 cm). Cover both sides with wrapping paper.

6 Open up the card. Tape the covered piece of paper in place behind the lifted butterfly.

7 Trace the butterfly pattern onto a piece of colored paper and cut out. Decorate the wings with sequins and glitter.

To finish off the card, lay a thin piece of ribbon along the folded edge and tie into a decorative bow on the outside.

8 Tape a small safety pin to the back of the butterfly and secure inside the card with a sticky pad.

15

Robin Hood Pouch

A simple-to-make money bag that can be hung from your belt or around your neck.

Materials

green material

3 feet (about 1 m) of cord

large wooden bead

painted cardboard leaf (from page 43)

1 Use a compass to draw an 8-inch (20-cm) diameter circle onto a piece of paper. Draw another circle within it 6½ inches (16 cm) in diameter.

2 Divide the inner circle up into 16 equal sections.

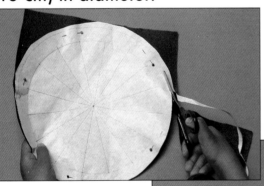

3 Trim down the paper around the circle and pin onto the material. Cut around the outer circle.

4 Before unpinning the paper, poke a pin through each of the 16 points marked on the inner circle and mark with a pen dot on the material. Unpin the paper.

5 Fold in half along each of the marked dots in turn and cut tiny slits, just large enough to thread the cord through to make a drawstring.

6 Begin to thread the cord through the holes. Thread on the painted leaf (use pattern on page 43) between the 8th and the 9th hole.

7 When you have threaded the cord through all the holes, pull the ends together and ease the material into a pouch shape.

8 Thread the cord ends through a snugly-fitting bead and knot the ends together. To close the pouch push the bead down.

You can also make a pretty party purse and decorate it with sequins and beads.

Mask on a Stick

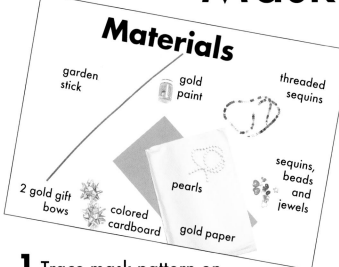

garden stick

gold paint

threaded sequins

pearls

sequins, beads and jewels

2 gold gift bows

colored cardboard

gold paper

You can use all sorts of bits and pieces to decorate these simple-to-make eye masks.

1 Trace mask pattern on page 46 onto thick cardboard to make a reuseable pattern. Draw around this pattern onto colored cardboard and cut out. Glue the mask onto the gold paper and trim around the edges. Cut out the eye holes.

2 Decorate the front of the mask with the sequins, jewels, beads and pearls.

3 Glue a gold gift bow to each corner.

18

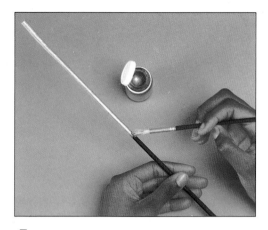

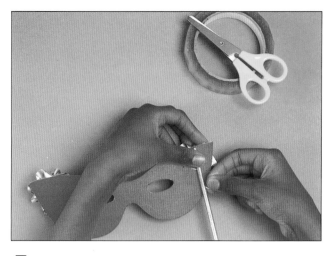

4 Cut the garden stick to about 1 foot (30 cm) long. Paint gold and leave to dry.

5 Tape the stick to one side on the back of the mask.

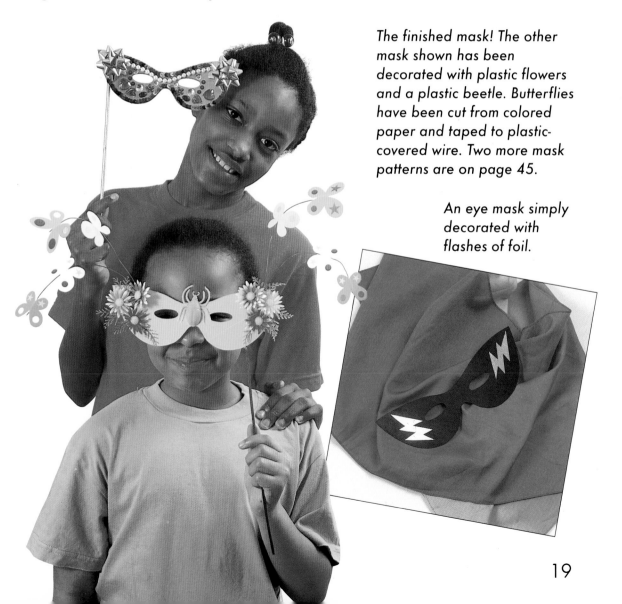

The finished mask! The other mask shown has been decorated with plastic flowers and a plastic beetle. Butterflies have been cut from colored paper and taped to plastic-covered wire. Two more mask patterns are on page 45.

An eye mask simply decorated with flashes of foil.

Materials

silver paper

silver stars

thin elastic

black paper

paper plate

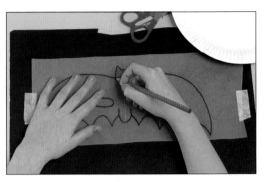

Batty

A super mask for Halloween.

1 Trace the bat pattern on page 46 onto the black paper. Cut out.

2 Cut the plate in half and paint the rounded side dark blue. Leave to dry.

3 Make a hole on either side of the plate and thread through the elastic. Knot both ends.

4 Glue the bat onto the painted side of the plate so that the eye holes come just below the cut edge. Leave the wing tips unglued so that the bat looks as if it is flying.

5 Cut a crescent moon from silver paper.

Adapt the look to become a living spider's web.

6 Stick the moon and the silver stars onto the blue plate above the bat.

Bird-of-Paradise

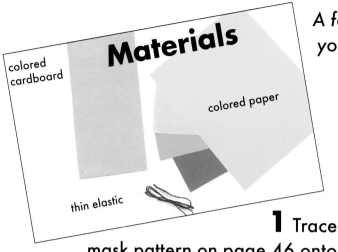

Materials

colored cardboard

colored paper

thin elastic

A fantastic mask that will make your budgie jealous!

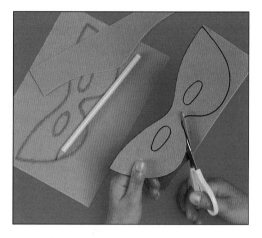

1 Trace mask pattern on page 46 onto colored cardboard and cut out.

! **2** Trace the beak pattern on page 46 onto colored paper and cut out. Ask an adult to score along the lines marked on the beak.

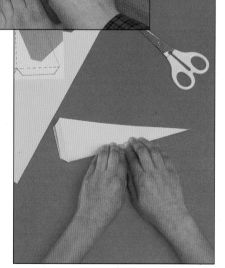

3 Fold the cardboard along the scored lines to make the beak shape.

4 Cut long and short spikes from colored paper. Glue these paper 'feathers' to the top corners of the mask, overlapping them as you go.

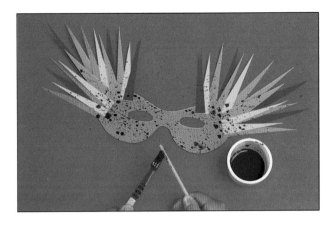

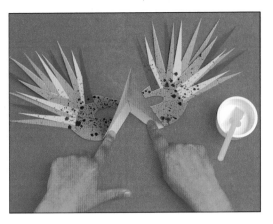

5 Dip a toothbrush into paint. Splatter the paint over the mask by gently pulling a paintbrush handle towards you along the head of the toothbrush. Leave to dry.

6 Put glue along the tabs on the beak and stick it to the center of the mask between the eye holes. To fit the elastic, see page 20 (step 3).

Why not try making other bird masks? For the toucan mask, use the beak pattern on page 46. Try fringing the edges of small pieces of paper to make the feathers.

Butterfly Wings

A beautiful butterfly mask that is sure to get you noticed.

Materials

2 pipe cleaners

sticker shapes

colored paper

thin elastic

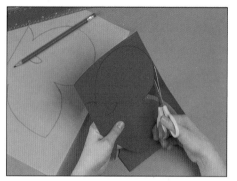

1 Trace the pattern on page 45 onto a piece of folded colored paper.

Cut out. Open the paper to reveal the butterfly.

2 Tear strips and circles from colored paper.

3 Glue the torn paper onto the front of the mask to decorate it. As you build up the pattern make sure that it is the same on both sides of the fold line.

4 Trim the ends of the paper strips to the shape of the butterfly wings.

5 To finish decorating the mask add sticker shapes to it.

6 Curl one end of the pipe cleaners around a pencil. Tape the uncurled ends to the back of the butterfly.

To fit the elastic to the finished mask, follow the instructions on page 20 (step 3).

Pasta Face

Dried pasta shapes arranged in a collage have been used to make this exciting tribal mask.

Materials

raffia

transparent plastic packaging

corrugated cardboard

thick paper

dried pasta shapes

1 Cut a large circle 1 foot (30 cm) in diameter from the corrugated cardboard. Cut 2 large holes 1½ inches (3.5 cm) apart in the center of the circle.

2 Cut 2 squares from the plastic packaging to fit over the eye holes and tape onto the back of the mask.

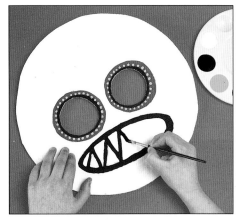

3 Paint the front of the mask white and leave to dry. Now paint around the eye holes and add a big mouth.

4 Stick pasta shapes all over the mask to make a pattern. Use hollow pasta tubes around the eyes.

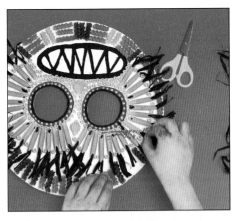

5 Cut the raffia into short lengths. Fold in half and push into the tubes of pasta.

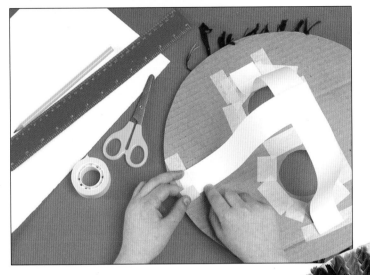

6 Tape a wide strip of paper about 20 inches (50 cm) long to either side of the eye holes on the back of the mask. Try on the mask to make sure it fits you. Adjust the paper strip if necessary.

7 Take a 1 foot (30 cm) long paper strip and tape one end of it to the center of the first strip, and the other end to the top edge of the mask.

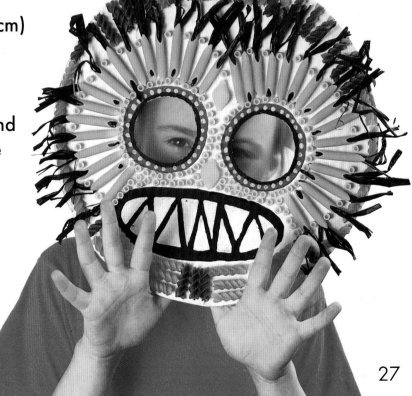

This mask should come with a warning 'Guaranteed to make you jump!'

Cowboy

Before riding off into the sunset, you'll need a pair of spurs for your boots and a horse, of course!

Horse

1 Stuff the sock with fabric scraps. Remove the adhesive backing from the plastic eyes, and stick them in place on the horse's head.

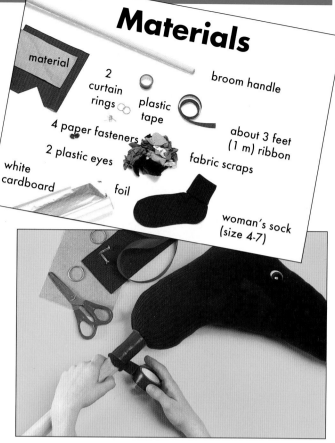

Materials

material

2 curtain rings

plastic tape

broom handle

4 paper fasteners

about 3 feet (1 m) ribbon

2 plastic eyes

fabric scraps

white cardboard

foil

woman's sock (size 4-7)

2 Push the broom handle into the sock and wind the tape securely around it.

! **3** Cut a fringe along one side of a strip of material and glue onto the horse's head. Cut out 2 large triangular material ears, fold in half and sew on.

4 Thread the rings onto ribbon long enough to go around the horse's nose with a ¾-inch (2-cm) overlap.

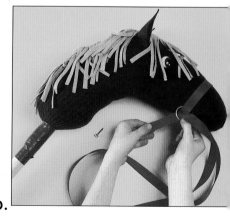

Glue the ribbon ends together and leave to dry. Thread the remaining ribbon onto the rings and fix with paper fasteners.

Spurs

5 Cut 2 stars (pattern on page 47) and 4 strips measuring 4 by 1 inches (10 x 2 cm) from the cardboard. Cover with foil.

To complete the look, wear a cowboy hat, checkered shirt, scarf and jeans; make a sheriff's badge using the pattern on page 47.

⚠ 6 Sandwich each star between 2 strips of cardboard and use an awl, or the point of some scissors, to make a hole through the 3 layers. Push a paper fastener through the hole and open out.

To fix the spurs to your boots, stick a piece of double-sided tape to the inside of the strips of cardboard. Remove the backing and press firmly onto the back of each boot.

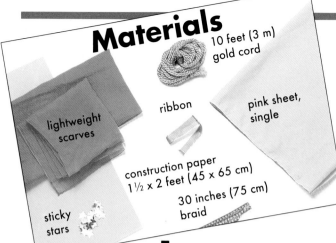

Materials

10 feet (3 m) gold cord

ribbon

pink sheet, single

lightweight scarves

construction paper 1½ x 2 feet (45 x 65 cm)

30 inches (75 cm) braid

sticky stars

Princess

A fairytale princess costume that can be adapted easily into a wise wizard outfit.

Cone hat

1 Fold the paper in half along its longest edge. Trace a triangle and cut out. You now have 2 paper triangles the same size.

2 Lay one triangle on top of the other, so that ¾ inch (1.5 cm) of the bottom triangle can be seen. Put double-sided tape along this edge, take off the backing and fold over onto the top triangle. Press firmly down. Turn over and repeat.

3 Trim the brim into a circle by cutting off the pointed ends. Decorate the cone with sticky stars all over and glue braid around the brim.

4 Snip off the top of the cone. Push the scarves into the hole and tape to the inside.

Robe

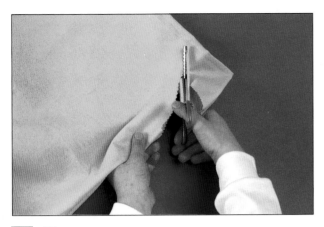

Tape ribbon to the inside to tie on the hat.

⚠ 5 Fold the sheet in half widthwise, then in half again lengthwise. To make an opening for your head, make a small triangular cut across the folded corner of the sheet with pinking shears.

Make a cloak from an old curtain. Thread with cord. Wrap around your shoulders and tie the cord under your chin.

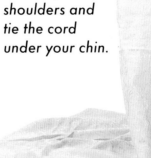

Adapt the look to become a wise wizard (star and moon patterns on page 47).

⚠ 6 Slip the sheet over your head. Wrap the cord around your waist, cross over your chest, and take over your shoulders. Cross the cord over your back and bring around to the front of your waist. Tie in a knot.

Knight

A few trusty snips of the scissors and some bold strokes of gluing will turn you into a brave knight.

Materials: pillowcase, red felt, ½ inch (1 cm) wide elastic, 2 silver-sprayed dishcloths, silver foil, silver cardboard, 5 paper fasteners, cardboard

Tunic

1 Make slits in the pillowcase for your arms and head. Cut 4 strips from the red felt. Snip a triangle into the end of each strip and glue onto the front of the tunic to make a cross.

Shield

2 Draw a shield onto the cardboard and cut out. Paint the front of the shield and leave to dry. Cut 2 pieces of elastic to fit around your forearm and staple into loops.

3 Thread the loops onto a cardboard strip and glue onto the back of the shield.

Helmet

4 Staple a silver dishcloth to the center of a silver cardboard band, measuring 24 by 2 inches (60 x 5 cm). Fit the band around your head and staple the ends together.

Slip the tunic over an outfit of gray sweatshirt, jogging pants, and rubber boots covered with silver foil. Wear a pair of gray woollen gloves.

5 Fix a 12 by 1½ inch (30 x 4 cm) strip of silver cardboard from one side of the headband to the other using paper fasteners. Now fix a strip measuring 20 by 1½ inches (50 x 4 cm) from the back to the front of the headband, leaving a bit of cardboard hanging down at the front.

6 Put the helmet on and ask a friend to mark the shape of your nose onto the nose bar. Cut out. Shape some foil into a dome to fit the inside of the helmet and tape in place. Staple the second dishcloth in place.

To finish off the shield, spray a large plastic lid with silver paint and glue to the center. To make a horse, see page 28.

Cut a 6-inch (15-cm) slit at the center of the bottom edge of the front of the tunic.

33

Christmas Present

Give your friends and family a surprise by wrapping yourself up for Christmas.

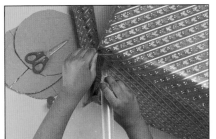

Materials

printed wrapping paper

large cardboard box

gift ribbon

Christmas card

metallic paper

⚠ 1 Cut the flaps from the box. Cut holes for your arms and head. Cover with wrapping paper.

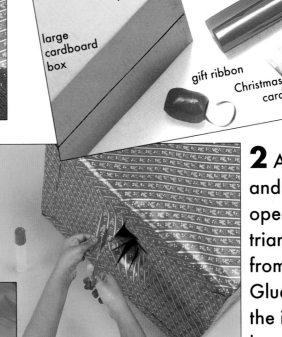

2 At the head and arm openings cut triangular tabs from the paper. Glue the tabs to the inside of the box.

3 For a decorative ribbon glue wide strips of metallic paper around the box.

4 Cut a large square of metallic paper. Fold over the edge of the paper by ¾ inch (2 cm) and press down. Turn over and fold over by ¾ inch (2 cm) again. Repeat until all the paper has been folded.

5 Fold in half and staple the top 2 edges together to make a fan. Put a length of double-sided tape along the bottom of the fan, remove the backing and press down firmly onto the box to the side of the head hole.

Tie the Christmas card gift tag around your wrist.

6 Punch a hole in the top left-hand corner of the Christmas card. Thread the ribbon through the hole.

Wear the Christmas present over an outfit of leotard and tights or sweatshirt and jogging pants.

To make a decoration for your hair, stick a bow onto a barrette. Curl lengths of thin metallic ribbon along closed scissor blades and tie to the barrette.

35

Cone People

Paper-mache simply means 'mashed paper.' You can model it into any shape with your hands or by applying it to a mold. But it is messy work and rubber gloves may be a good idea.

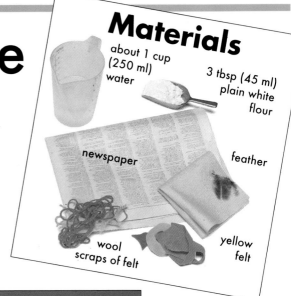

Materials

about 1 cup (250 ml) water

3 tbsp (45 ml) plain white flour

newspaper

feather

wool scraps of felt

yellow felt

1 Tear the newspaper into lengths about 1 inch (3 cm) wide. Tear these strips again into small stamp-size pieces. Put into a container.

!2 Cover the torn paper with hot water and leave to soak overnight.

3 Take handfuls of paper and squeeze the water out. Place the squeezed-out paper into another bowl. Empty the water from the container.

4 Put the flour into a mixing bowl. Add the water slowly and mix to a smooth, creamy paste.

5 Put the squeezed paper back into the bucket a little at a time, mixing it with small amounts of paste until it becomes a smooth pulp. You may need to mix more paste.

6 Take a handful of paper-mache and work into a cone. Smooth the sides. Leave to dry in a warm, dry place for several days.

7 Paint the cone with 2 coats of bright paint. When dry, paint on the eyes, nose and mouth.

8 Glue some short strands of wool around the sides and back of the head, about 2 inches (4 cm) from the top of the cone. Cut out a felt loop large enough to fit over the top of the cone just above the hair. Add a feather.

If you cannot make a cone shape, make one that is rounded at the top instead, just like the little red one shown here.

Paper-Mache Boat

A plastic bottle cut in half makes a perfect mold for making the hull of a boat from mashed paper.

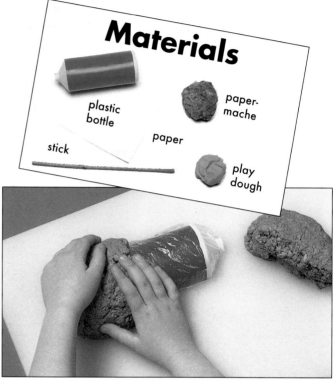

Materials

plastic bottle

paper-mache

paper

stick

play dough

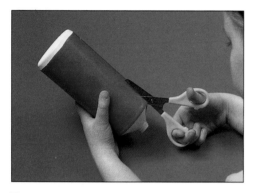

1 Cut a small plastic bottle in half lengthwise. Cover one half with plastic wrap.

2 Spread paper-mache evenly over the half bottle mold until it is about ¼ inch (½ cm) thick. Leave to dry in a warm, dry place for several days.

3 Carefully ease the bottle and plastic wrap from the paper-mache. Leave for another day or two to let the inside dry out thoroughly.

4 Paint the boat inside and out. Several coats of paint may be needed. Once the paint has dried, the hull can be varnished.

5 To make a sail, cut a piece of paper 10 by 8 inches (24 cm x 20 cm) and color with felt pens.

6 Punch a hole at the center top and center bottom of the sail. Slip the sail onto the stick.

7 Take a lump of play dough and press it firmly into the center of the boat. Push the stick mast into the play dough.

To make your boat into a Viking ship, cut out and decorate some circles for shields. Stick them along each side of the boat.

39

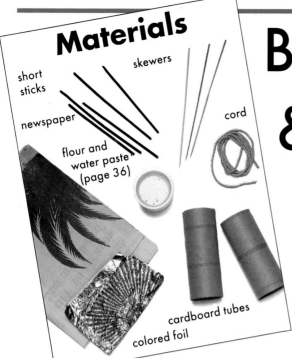

Materials

short sticks

skewers

newspaper

flour and water paste (page 36)

cord

cardboard tubes

colored foil

Beads, Beads & More Beads

Lots of different beads to make. Thread them onto string, wool, elastic, or even an old shoelace.

Paper-mache pulp beads

1 Tear newspaper into stamp-size squares and put into a bowl. Cover with warm water and leave to soak for 24 hours.

2 Squeeze the water from the paper and drain. Add a little paste and mix well to form a mush.

3 Take small balls of mush and form into large beads around the short sticks.

! **4** Slide the balls carefully off the sticks and place onto an old baking tray. Leave in the oven overnight on its lowest setting to dry out thoroughly.

5 Thread the beads back onto the sticks. Push the end of the sticks into a lump of play dough, making sure that the beads are not touching each other. Decorate with paint, then varnish. Slide the beads off the sticks once dry.

Paper beads

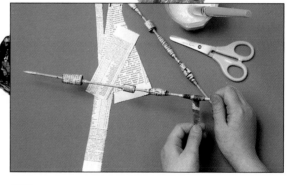

6 Cut newspaper into strips of different widths and lengths, including some pennant-shaped strips. The longer the strip the larger the bead will be.

7 Put paste on one side of the paper strips and wind glue-side down around the skewers. Gently pull the beads off the skewers and leave to dry.

Continues on next page

8 Thread the beads back onto the skewers and stick into a ball of play dough. Paint the beads all over and leave to dry. Use several different base colors.

9 Decorate the beads by painting on patterns in contrasting colors and by sticking on strips of colored foil. When dry, slide the beads off the skewers.

Cardboard beads

10 Paint and decorate the tubes. When dry, cover with a light coat of varnish and leave to dry.

11 Cut open the tubes and paint the insides black. When dry, cut into ¾-inch (2-cm) wide sections.

12 Tape the painted sections into circles once again, linking them as you go to make a chain.

Patterns

Here are all the patterns you will need to make the projects in this book. Simply trace around the required outline using tracing paper or greaseproof paper, and transfer onto paper or cardboard. It is also a good idea to make a cardboard pattern that you can re-use time and time again. Lay a piece of tracing paper over the required pattern. Draw around the outline with a pencil. Turn over the tracing paper and scribble over the pencil outline. Turn the tracing paper over once again and lay down onto a piece of thick cardboard. Carefully draw around the pencil outline. Remove the tracing paper. The outline of the traced shape on the cardboard may be quite faint. Go over it with black felt pen. Cut out and label the cardboard pattern and keep it in a safe place. Use it to draw around as many times as is needed onto paper, cardboard or material.

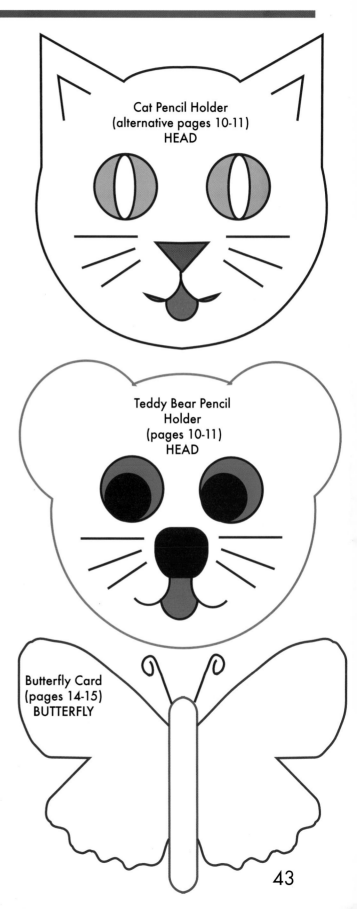

Cat Pencil Holder
(alternative pages 10-11)
HEAD

Teddy Bear Pencil
Holder
(pages 10-11)
HEAD

Robin Hood Pouch
(pages 16-17)
LEAF

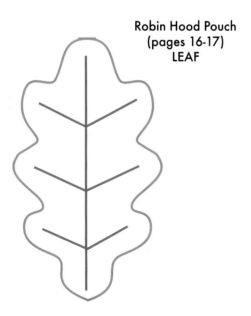

Butterfly Card
(pages 14-15)
BUTTERFLY

43

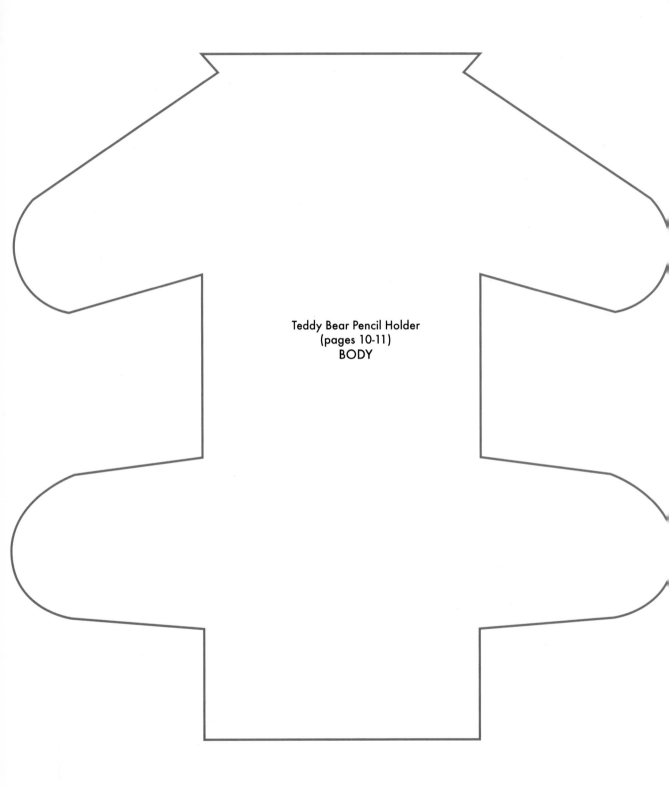

Teddy Bear Pencil Holder
(pages 10-11)
BODY

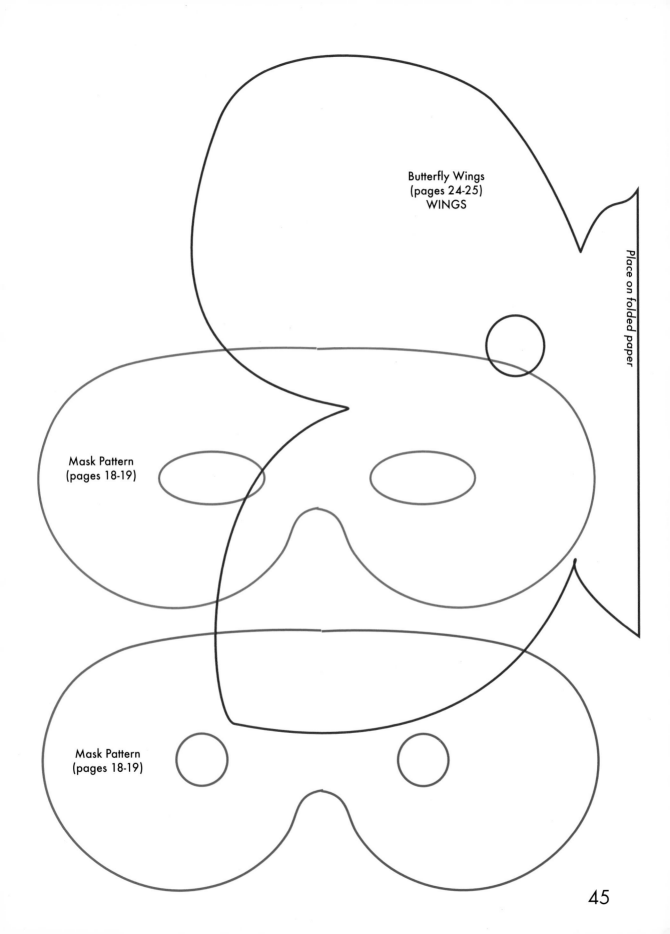

Butterfly Wings
(pages 24-25)
WINGS

Place on folded paper

Mask Pattern
(pages 18-19)

Mask Pattern
(pages 18-19)

45

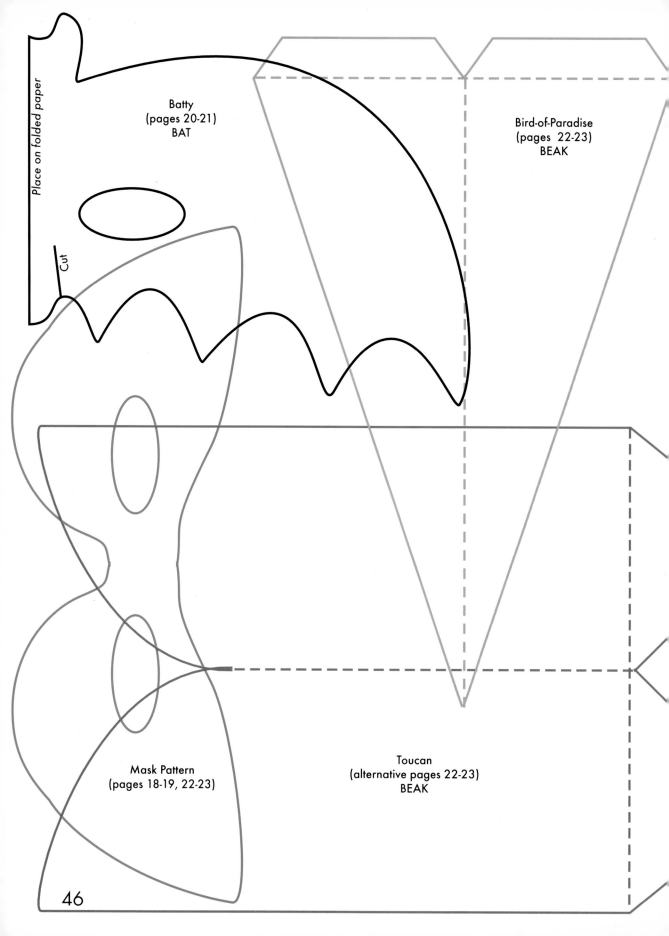

Place on folded paper

Cut

Batty
(pages 20-21)
BAT

Bird-of-Paradise
(pages 22-23)
BEAK

Mask Pattern
(pages 18-19, 22-23)

Toucan
(alternative pages 22-23)
BEAK

46

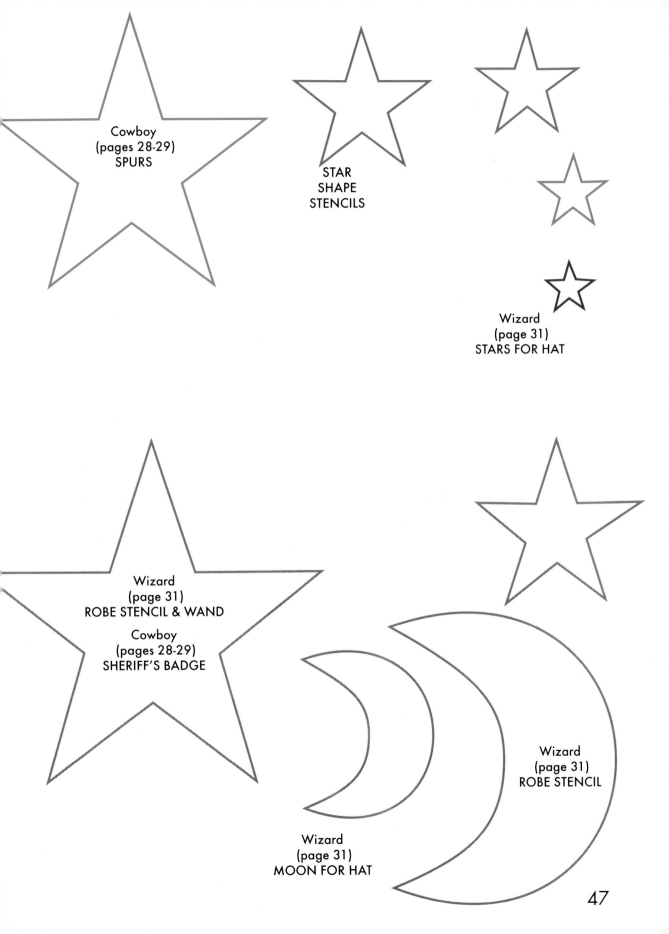

Cowboy
(pages 28-29)
SPURS

STAR
SHAPE
STENCILS

Wizard
(page 31)
STARS FOR HAT

Wizard
(page 31)
ROBE STENCIL & WAND

Cowboy
(pages 28-29)
SHERIFF'S BADGE

Wizard
(page 31)
ROBE STENCIL

Wizard
(page 31)
MOON FOR HAT

47

Advice to Parents

This book is full of exciting ideas for turning simple materials, or even junk, into interesting and beautiful items children will enjoy making again and again. Most of the projects in this book can be made with things that can be found around the home: food packages, plastic bottles, old sheets and pillowcases, odd socks, cloth scraps, dishcloths, to name just a few. Some of the projects are quick to make, others need some advance preparation, so consider planning ahead. Work on several projects at a time, so that your child does not lose interest waiting for paint or varnish to dry, or dough to bake. For making dress-up costumes, use old clothing or linen items, but don't rush out to the shops with your checkbook. After all, the magical thing about dressing up is that children can transform themselves into a king or queen, a hero or a heroine, with their imagination alone. These projects aim to help them bring their imaginings to life. Some of the projects show how the patterns (found on pages 43 to 47) can be used in a slightly different way to create variations. Encourage your child to further adapt the patterns, or create new ones, to design masks, dress-up costumes, etc. which are uniquely theirs. The information on this page is designed to help you to encourage your child to get the most from these projects.

Tools and Materials

Felt pens A set of felt pens is a good idea for adding fine decorative details to models, masks and paper dress-up items.

Double-sided tape This tape is very strong. It is rather expensive but worth every penny. If you use it carefully it will go a long way. It is a perfect alternative to glue on fabric when a temporary join is all that is required. It comes in rolls in various widths and can be bought at office supply stores and arts and crafts shops.

Glue Solvent-free white glue, or glue stick tubes are recommended as they are versatile, clean, strong and safe.

Paint From a small selection of paints—red, yellow, blue, black and white—all other colors can be obtained by mixing. Encourage your child to explore color mixing for herself. Poster paints are ideal for painting all the projects in this book. Always ensure that paint has dried before going on to the next step in the project. Add a drop of dishwashing liquid to the paint when painting on plastic. Always help your child when using spray paints. Put small items in a cardboard box and spray. Larger items should be sprayed outdoors if possible.

Varnish A light coat of varnish will give completed items a shiny finish and a protective coat that will help them to last longer. You should buy non-toxic varnish that is suitable for children to use, available at most arts and crafts stores. Always ensure that the varnish has completely dried before adding any other decorations.

Paper and cardboard Try to keep both white and colored paper, construction paper and cardboard in the house. Reuse and recycle paper and cardboard whenever possible. Make use of leftover bits of wallpaper, for example. Colored construction paper and cardboard can be expensive: old cereal boxes, folded flat, are perfect when thin to medium cardboard is needed. Simply paint the unprinted side of the cardboard whatever color is required.

Scissors For safety's sake, children should use small scissors with round-ended metal blades and plastic handles. These will not cut cardboard or fabric easily and this is best done by an adult. You should cut cardboard with a precision knife. Use a metal ruler to provide a straight cutting edge. If you do not have a cutting mat, use an old chopping board or some thick corrugated cardboard to protect the work surface beneath.

Paper-mache

Paper-mache is a cheap and versatile modeling material made from old newspapers and a flour and water paste. To make this smooth, slightly runny paste you will need approximately 3 tablespoons (45 ml) of plain white flour to about 1 cup (250 ml) of water. Gradually add the water to the flour and mix well. Make sure that the paper-mache items have dried out completely before decorating. This will take at least 24 hours in a dry, warm place.

Play Dough and Salt Dough

Play dough can be bought readymade from toy shops and some office supply stores. It is also incredibly simple to make and a recipe has been given on page 4 of this book. Play dough that has been stored in the refrigerator may require a few drops of oil to be kneaded into it to make it pliable. Salt dough items can be baked hard in the oven, decorated and varnished, so that they can be kept forever. Salt dough is best made the day before it is required. Store in a plastic bag in the refrigerator. Before using, knead well on a lightly floured board. Before baking salt dough models, brush lightly with a little water to give a good finish. Place items on a lightly greased or non-stick cookie sheet. NOTE: Salt dough cannot be cooked in a microwave oven!

A child-size rolling pin is advisable for rolling out play dough, salt dough and clay prior to shaping or cutting. For cutting, children can use a round-ended knife or modeling tool, bottle caps, jar lids and cookie cutters. NOTE: Care should be taken with metal cookie cutters: if accidentally placed the wrong way up and pressed hard, they could cut the hand. Encourage children to create a variety of textures on the surface of dough and clay, experimenting with all sorts of household items from fork prongs to empty spools.